Social Media

The Ultimate Guide to Transforming Your Brand with Social Media

(Featuring a 7 Step Action Plan for Beginners)

Brad Jones

ISBN-13: 978-1517471323
ISBN-10: 151747132X

CONTENTS

INTRODUCTION

When you set out to do something for the first time, it can seem daunting. No matter what the activity or task, you are essentially starting from scratch. You notice that others are doing it very well, but can't help wondering how you will ever learn what it's all about. Internet marketing with success can seem like an impossible task to many people. Even if you are quite a wiz on social media, it doesn't necessarily mean that you have the foggiest idea on how to market yourself and your brand.

You might be thinking to yourself "Social media marketing plan? How the heck do I make one of those?" Don't worry, because this book is going to take you through all of the information that you will need.

INTRODUCING SOCIAL MEDIA

If you are not totally sold on the whole idea of marketing through social media, the following chapter is aimed at changing your mind.

There are a lot of different social media platforms out there, and it's practically impossible to try them all. To make this all easier, they are listed and discussed in the chapter **"The Most Effective Social Media Platform for You"**. If you think that you'd rather try something else, be sure to do a lot of research into that platform and don't just start using one because it was recommended to you by a friend.

Once you have decided which of the social media platforms you want to try out, the chapter **"10 Powerful Social Media Strategies"** has some top advice on how to make your marketing efforts effective. Be sure to read each of them carefully, and think about how you can put them into action.

No matter how much good you do, making just a few major mistakes can have a terrible toll on your efforts. That is why the chapter **"Top 10 Mistakes People Make on Social Media, and How to Avoid Them"** is a must-read. There are lots of mistakes you can make using social media, knowing some of the most common mistakes can help to steer clear of trouble.

Once you have a firm understanding of the rest of the information in this book, you will need to put things into action. That's where knowing how to make a good social media marketing plan will help. No matter how, without a solid action plan you are less likely to see your goals become realities. The chapter **"Putting It All Together: Your Social Media Plan"** will guide you through this process.

WHY SOCIAL MEDIA IS SO INFLUENTIAL

Having a great website simply is not enough anymore. The digital world requires successful businesses to go beyond that these days. That means expanding into social media platforms, such as the widely known Facebook and Twitter. In fact, these days it pays to go beyond the most popular platforms, into the realms of LinkedIn and Blogging. If you're not familiar with the inner workings of all these platforms, that's fine. It's really not that difficult to learn, and there are lots of tutorials around on the Internet. However, this book will assume that you have at least a basic understanding of using social media.

So, why exactly do you need to increase your focus on social media marketing? Isn't that for companies with no advertising budgets, like the kind that are run out of people's garages? Yes, and no. There are lots of reasons to use social media to grow your brand, and the cost factor is just one of them. Don't take my word for it though. Check out more reasons below.

Increased Sales

It shouldn't come as a surprise that putting your message in front of customers will lead to more sales. Social media is perfect for keeping your brand and message in plain sight for your customers. It also gives companies the opportunity to provide incentives for making purchases. You can share special deals or discount coupons, so that your followers will see them. People are always looking for great deals online. You might be surprised to find just how many people share your codes and make purchases.

It Costs Nothing

How can you possibly say no to something so great, when it doesn't cost a thing. Creating and using your business profiles on these sites will not cost you anything. However, if you want to use premium services, such as sponsored posts and advertisements, it will cost you. The prices are still very good, and many businesses find that it is worthwhile.

Would you like to have someone else take care of social media for you? There are special PR agencies that can do all the work. It can cost you up to several thousand dollars per month for a good agency, but the money you can potentially make in return will be greater.

The Playing Field is Level

If you are a larger company, this might not be such great news. Because of the almost non-existent costs to entry, social media marketing lets even the smallest businesses compete with the big guys. Those who can excel on the Internet are often the best at marketing. You don't need millions of dollars to get people's attention. However, because of this, you will need to be extremely clever with how you approach your social media marketing campaigns. There is plenty of competition, so make sure to do things right.

Instant Damage Control

When someone has a problem with your business, it can be quite harmful. When a product or service is not up to standard, it is important that you know right away. Luckily, people regularly post feedback on social media sites. Many of them don't just want to tell their friends and family about their grievance either. They want to make sure that you see it too. This means that you will know about any problems right away.

Responding to the complaints of your customers are important. Instead of letting them go around telling others how "terrible" your company is, you can activate damage control immediately.

Connect with Your Target Demographic Directly

What's the problem with one way advertising, where you are just showing things to people? It's difficult to find out anything about your target market, or how well they are receiving your marketing campaigns. That is one of the neatest things about sites like Twitter and Facebook. There is a ton of interaction going on, between all sorts of people. You can connect with your customers and find out what their thoughts are. There is no need to even ask, because people are happy to share what they think about all kinds of things. You will be able to alter your marketing strategy according to what your targeted demographic market is telling you online.

Don't Get Left Behind

Face it, your competitors are out there posting on Pinterest and Tweeting to their customers. The earlier you begin to build yourself a social media fan base, the better chance you will have of controlling the market. Getting in early is often the easiest way to do things, provided that you make the right choices. However, trying to catch up with other companies that already have a head start can be difficult. If you wait too long, you will probably need to spend more money to catch up. If you don't believe me, go and search for your competitors on a few popular social media platforms. Are they already using them to interact with people? You better need to get started then!

Spy on Competition

This isn't really spying, since all the information is displayed publicly. If you want to know what your competitors are up to, following their social media profiles is practically essential these days. To be sure that you are not left behind with any trends, you need to keep your fingers on the pulse. This is the kind of information that marketers from the past would only have dreamed of. Why would you let something like that slip by you, especially when it's free and easy to do?

People Want to Listen

The public has become pretty good at ignoring advertising. After all, it is basically everywhere we go. When it comes to social media, people are still eager to hear what you have to tell them. Social networks are still largely seen as something for the average person. Your messages are likely to be seen as social interactions, rather than advertisements and their use as marketing tools is growing.

Reach out to New Customers

You might think you have already tapped all the customer bases out there. Think again, because social media will help you find customers that you didn't think existed. You can search for people using huge databases of individuals, groups and businesses. After narrowing down your searches, you are almost guaranteed to find new potential customers.

People will also use social media platforms to track you down. If you are offering goods or services that people want, they are likely to find you. Simply by maintaining your presence, and marketing yourself in smart ways, you can reach out and grab hold of loads of new customers.

THE MOST EFFECTIVE SOCIAL MEDIA PLATFORM FOR YOU

There is no "best" social media platform for any particular business. You need to select one that will best allow you to connect with your targeted audience. It also comes down to what type of media you want to produce, depending on what will suit your business. If you think that you can excel on all of the popular social media platforms, you might be getting a bit carried away. That kind of thing takes a huge amount of resources.

Rather than just doing an average job of marketing yourself on a lot of different platforms, why not choose to focus on fewer. That might be easier said than done, because you must select the most effective ones for your business. There are way too many social media services out there to list here. Instead, below are the ones that you should be looking into.

Facebook

Have you heard of this one? You really should have, because it's been the number one social media site for many years. The pure amount of people using it makes it a powerful marketing tool. It is fairly safe to assume that most of your customers will have Facebook accounts, many of whom regularly uses theirs.

You can accurately target who will see your posts, and what you would like to share. This will allow you to tailor exactly how you want to present your business to people, unlike with some other platforms. It takes time to build up a good following on Facebook, and there is loads of competition. However, you can interact directly with people, and reply immediately.

Many people make the mistake of trying to sell to people through Facebook. They are missing the whole point of this medium. You should aim to show people what your company is all about. Give them a personal touch, while being social and friendly. You need to act more like a "mom and pop" business on Facebook. No one wants to interact with a big, faceless corporation here as many use the platform to seek out human interaction.

Use posts, images, and even videos, to show customers the people behind the logo. They are happy to see pictures of your family and friends, or the company picnic. If they can see that your business really cares about people on an individual level, it's going to be a lot easier to sell to them.

Twitter

Twitter is somewhat like a constant series of text messages, and the format has become very popular with users. Instead of focusing on making a user profile page that works like a mini website it is more immediate. Posts on Twitter are called "tweets". When you make one, be ready for people to respond quickly. This makes it ideal for sending out news, special deals, updates, and requests for opinions. This platform really is best for companies who wish to share things directly on a regular basis.

Twitter is not a great choice for people who want to upload media for others to look at later. Sure, you can share links to images, videos, websites, etc., but the focus is primarily placed upon text messages. There is even a limit of 140 characters per message (including spaces), to ensure that people don't clog up the feeds of others. Do you like to create long-winded posts, with lots of information and media, then Twitter is not going to be the ideal social media platform for your business.

You can message people directly, and they can do the same. This is done with a special system of tags and text shortcuts that are placed directly in tweets. You can make these messages private, but Twitter lacks all the special messaging services that many other sites have. Due to their dramatic differences, and combined popularity, Twitter and Facebook work well together as part of a marketing plan.

YouTube

YouTube is an amazing platform for people who have videos to share. It is the largest video sharing platform in the world at the moment, and has been so for a while now. Users can create their own accounts that work like video channels. You can actually have several channels, making up a type of mini network for your business. Videos work well, because the public often prefer to watch videos over reading something. Even videos that are nothing more than text and music tend to do well.

If you are willing to create some videos for your business, or pay a professional to do so, YouTube can be valuable. However, unless you wish to do this, the platform has little to offer you. Since YouTube is owned by Google, you can be sure that they will give preferences to user profiles in their search engine. Please note that this has not been confirmed, but is widely agreed that YouTube pages do very well in Google.

LinkedIn

This is the social media network for professionals. It is best related to more traditional types of business networking. Everything has simply been transferred into a digital, online medium. It is a great way for people to build new connections, specifically in the world of business. It never hurts to have more people in your professional network, so LinkedIn is usually a good choice for most businesses.

Your goal on this network isn't to try and sell to people. In fact, many of your targeted customers will not have their own accounts, unless they are active in the business community or perhaps looking for new jobs. People do participate in discussions. It is a great place to go to discuss business, ask people for some help or even to show off your expertise, it is a great way for networking and for impressing people.

You can create an extensive profile, for yourself and your business. This can include past experience, professional goals, and various things that show others what you are all about. On the other hand it certainly isn't the right place to share pictures of your family or talk about hobbies. While many individuals do those things to build themselves up as relatable people, it doesn't work as well for businesses.

You can use LinkedIn to find new employees or freelancers, since many of them will have their own profiles. It is also a great place to do research on your competition. By following other companies within your niche, you can stay ahead of them in many ways.

Blogging

This isn't a specific social media site or service. A blog is a type of Internet Journal. The name comes from "web log", which is what they were originally, and still largely are. Think of Blogs as personal websites, where people can write posts about anything they like. Many individuals use them to write about their thoughts, opinions, daily lives or hobbies. Likely, due to this very personal way of sharing, people have started to adore Blogs. There are a lot of bloggers who make plenty of money on their own Blogs and businesses have started to take notice of this trend. There are now many professional Blogs out there.

The trick with a Blog is to make it very personal, relatable and human. Even though your Blog will relate to your business and industry, people want to know who is doing the writing. It's a good idea to find someone with a great personality to operate your Blog. You can hire a professional to maintain yours or just get an employee do it. You can share videos and images on your Blog, but there has to be a personal touch to whatever you do. Don't focus on putting the hard sell on people. It also helps to provide valuable content. This value can come in the form of entertainment, information or something more personal.

Video Blogs, referred to as "Vlogs", are gaining popularity. They are essentially the Blog format turned into a video medium. Instead of bloggers writing their posts, they create videos and upload them. YouTube is the most popular platform for Video Blogs.

Instagram

This social media platform is quite different from many others. It revolves around a mobile app, which is used for taking and sharing photos. Users can also share videos of up to 15 seconds in length. It was first launched in 2013, when there wasn't much else like it out there. With over 200 million people using the service each month, you will find lots of potential customers.

Does your company have a lot of visual media to share? If you can show off your products, as with a retail or manufacturing business, Instagram might be just what you need. There are lots of great opportunities for smaller companies too. The app truly is about giving power to individuals, who otherwise might never have their videos and photos seen. It comes with simple editing features, which allow users to upload some great looking media. Even if you have little-to-zero money in your advertising budget, you can benefit from Instagram. If you are able to spend even a small amount of money, you can then get some superb results.

Unlike Facebook, Twitter, and LinkedIn this platform is designed for visual sharing. You can create your own brand videos or images and show them to your customers. However, you should remember that photos are what this service is really about. If you are only interested in sharing videos, you should definitely focus on using YouTube, or at least both platforms.

Pinterest

As with Instagram, this platform is directed toward those who have visual media to share. The idea behind the service is to allow users to connect to people who have similar interests. Users' profiles work kind of like vision boards. Using their own choice of theme, people can create their own "board". When they come across something on the World Wide Web that they wish to share or save for later, they can use the "Pin It" button.

Pinned items are known as "Pins". They also don't have to be just images either. Users can pin videos, or even discussions. The pinned items can be divided into different categories on a board. For example, ideas for wedding themes and decorations can go onto a "Wedding" section.

Users can follow other people, as well as company brands. If they see someone pin something that takes their interest, they can choose to "re-pin" that item. It's easy to see how a business could use this to build up a rapidly expanding following, especially if they had a lot of visually appealing things to share.

10 MOST POWERFUL SOCIAL MEDIA STRATEGIES

Act Like Each Social Media Platform is its Own Entity

All of the profiles on each different channel will probably be quite similar. However, you must remember to treat them as unique entities. Even if you are sharing a lot of the same content, you need to alter strategies for sharing it on different platforms.

As an example, compare Twitter to Pinterest. Twitter is a lot less visual, and posts need to be relatively short. You can share links to more visual media, but the focus is clearly on text messages. Now, take Pinterest. People are looking for things like pictures and videos here. Imagine that you are sharing news about your new store opening. While you need to get the same basic information across on each of these social media platforms, you would do it in very different ways.

For Twitter, you might just text that the new store has opened, give some details about its location and inviting people to come and check it out. For Pinterest, you would want to show images of the storefront, as well as some of your displays and products. It would probably also help to share images of your happy employees in the store.

You can see how the same information needs to be shared in different ways. That's why it pays to treat each of your social media marketing channels as individual entities, within the same brand umbrella.

Make a Plan and Follow Through

Unless you have a solid plan, you might end up wasting loads of time. You might be producing some excellent content, but allowing it to go past most people's attention. There are a lot of things that you can include in your plan. It will all be explained in more detail in the chapter

"Putting It All Together: Your Social Media Plan." Let's say that you plan to use Twitter as your primary social media marketing platform. How many tweets do you think you will need to publish every day? It can really be as simple as deciding that you will publish five per day. That isn't a whole lot, and it might seem like no plan is required. However, without setting out what you need to do, it can be easy to stray from the intended path.

Of course, your plan might be more complicated than the example given above. Before you start making your plan, it helps to do some research to find out what the competition is doing on the social media sites. Just look at their profiles and see what they are getting up to. Don't assume that your plan is going to work.

Once you have your plan — stick with it. It is okay to modify the plan, but you can't just toss it aside and start doing things at random. That is when it starts to become risky and potential failure is lurking.

Customer Service is Essential

If someone posts a comment on your company's Facebook page, and they never get a reply, how do you think they will feel? It is quite possible that they will go to a competitor, who can offer them better service. People hate being ignored on social media. If you fail to communicate with people, they might think that you don't care about their business. In contrast, if you were to answer them promptly, with something helpful and thoughtful, they might be eager to do business with you.

This all comes back to making your brand something that is distinctly human. Keep in mind, that's what social media is primarily about — humans interacting with each other. If you can't offer that personal touch, your brand and business will seem like an uncaring, faceless company.

Not only does good customer service help you to hold onto customers and draw new ones in, but it gives you a chance to display your authority.

Answering questions and giving advice is a sure way to build your brand as a leader in your business niche. Likewise, if you want to take care of potentially damaging feedback, you need to stay on top of answering and replying to customers' posts.

Share Content Multiple Times

Have you ever wondered why some brands share their posts more than once? It might seem a bit redundant, since their followers have surely had a chance to see them already. There are, however, several reasons why you should follow this tactic.

Sharing content more than once will increase your chances of getting more traffic. This is one of the more obvious advantages. While it is likely that sub-sequential postings of the same content will not be as effective as the first time you shared them, they can still be beneficial.

If you share things once, you are only reaching out to people in certain time zones. Don't forget that building a brand often means gathering followers from all over the world. This is important, even for businesses that are locally based. You can, after all, never have too many fans and followers, or too much exposure.

You shouldn't repost things immediately or even in the same month. You can re-share things that were created some time ago, provided that they are still relevant. This way, many people will not realize that you are reusing old content. Make sure that you modify the actual post a bit though, just in case people do catch on. This is a great tactic for getting more followers, without actually creating more new material to share.

Use A/B Testing

This technique will be much easier if you share each posts multiple times. When you do re-share, try out a different headline and different post text. Not only will this shake things up and keep your posts from looking the same, it will also allow you to test out what types of posts and headlines give the best results. It's important to do this type of "split" testing, so that you can experiment with different tactics. It also gives you a chance to choose the methods that are working the best.

If you are going to do split testing, be sure to reduce the effects of varying circumstances. Try to publish each test post at around the same time of the same day. About an hour apart is a good rule of thumb. This means that you will be reaching similar people, in similar parts of the world, on the same days. You don't want to post one test item on a Sunday and the other on a Wednesday. There's no way that you can tell which headline and text does best, since users activity can vary so much between these days.

Track Your Data

A lot of people try to avoid this task. Tracking your data is widely considered time consuming and somewhat mundane. While those things can be true, it doesn't need to use up much of your time. Even if you just allocate a handful of hours from each month, you can make sure to stay on top of data tracking for your social media platforms.

Choose the specific metrics that you feel are most important to your brand and marketing plan. The first day of each month is an ideal time to do this, so mark it on your calendar now. Next, you will need to decide which statistics should be monitored and recorded. Some commonly used metrics are growth of followers, amount of posts, page views, clicks through to your product or website, impressions (the amount of page loads you get), post shares, post likes, post comments, etc.

Once again, when you are deciding what metrics to track, think of each social media platform as an individual entity. Whatever you do, make sure that you actually record and archive all of your data. It might seem unnecessary at the moment, but you never know when it could come in handy. You can compare your data to that of competitors and see how well you are doing.

Spend Some Money

You can't escape the fact that people often get what they pay for. If you can dedicate many work hours to maintaining a beneficial social media marketing plan, that's wonderful. However, it is usually a good idea to take out that wallet and hand over some cash. One of the leading growth areas in the world of online marketing is paid advertisements on social media.

Take Facebook as an example. It hasn't been that long since the company unveiled their paid marketing scheme. It basically gives brands a way to target and manage how their posts are seen. That is, of course, if they are willing to pay for that privilege. Say what you want about this money making plan, but it certainly gives great results to businesses that take advantage.

The rapidly expanding selection of advertising features on this platform, and many others, can give you a big leg-up with your own marketing. You can choose exactly what types of people should see your ads, and even elect to only pay for real results.

While ads on social media might bother many users, they are only so prevalent because they get results. If you want to give your social media marketing efforts a boost, be sure to consider using paid advertising. It is a lot more affordable than you might think.

Host Events through Social Media

This is a great way to build a huge, highly loyal base of fans. Hosting online social media events can help to make your customers feel valued, while increasing your visibility among the Internet community.

A simple type of event is "Fan Day". This basically involves letting your followers network with each other and enjoy a little free marketing of their own. Once a week, or as often as you like, give your fans a chance to share links to their own pages, on your page. This is a great way to build your own network as you find new businesses. There is a chance that you will draw in new fans as well. People will share the word around to their friends and contacts, telling them about the opportunity. They will also view you as a caring and helpful member of the community. Everyone wins, right?

While you could do this type of thing once a week, you might want to hold off a little longer. If you do it too often, the impact will be somewhat lost. Once every two-to-four weeks might be a better idea, especially if you don't have a huge number of fans yet. That will give people more time to get the word out and for interest to build up.

Use Images on Updates

If you are posting regularly and people are not commenting on, sharing or liking your posts, you are not successfully marketing yourself. In order to make sure that your brand's posts are seen often, you need to create a lot of fan engagement. An easy way to do this is with images.

On many platforms, like Facebook for example, using plain text is a wonderful way to be ignored. Take a look at the amount of posts containing some type of image. Often, they are nothing but an image and a few words. There are even many "images" that really are just text, with some sort of colored background. It doesn't seem to matter if the image actually contains anything more, because people still respond positively.

If you can use a large, colorful image, that's great. Even if you are on a platform that only allows smaller thumbnails, go ahead and make use of them. The more visually stimulating you can be with your online marketing content, the better. Otherwise, you run the risk of users overlooking your posts, in favor of the flashier brands.

Use Influencers to Get Noticed

"Influencers" are people who hold power over large amounts of users. They are the big guys in the social media world. When these people draw attention to something, a lot of people sit up and pay attention. It can be pretty difficult to get these influential people to take notice of your brand. That's why you need to publish posts that will get them to take notice.

At least some of your posts should be created to draw attention of influencers in your industry. Don't go overboard catering to them, or you might risk losing your followers. You don't have to always share your own content either. You can re-share posts that you know will be popular. This makes it seem that you are ahead of the game and paying attention to trends before they get big. It will also increase the chances that influencers will see something that you have shared, and draw attention to your own company profile. Use these tactics carefully, to avoid becoming nothing more than a re-sharing, rehashing "wannabe".

TOP 10 MISTAKES PEOPLE MAKE ON SOCIAL MEDIA AND HOW TO AVOID THEM

Paying for Followers and Likes

Yes, you certainly can buy likes and followers on many social network sites. Even if it's not offered as an official service, there are more shady ways to do this. Before you think about it any further, realize now that it's a terrible idea. Do you think that those followers will help your business? You can almost guarantee that your paid-for followers will not care about your brand in the least.

The overall quality of your followers as a group will drop. In turn, the effectiveness of your posts will also drop. Even after reading this, you might still be tempted to pay to increase your likes and followers — but don't do it. There are so many better ways to go about building up a social media fan-base.

Doing Nothing But Advertising

There are plenty of ways that this can bother people. First, most people just hate seeing ads in any form. They are using social media to connect with their friends and family, while making new contacts along the way. Seeing a stream of posts about how great your product is, or why people simply must check out your website, will anger them. Using social media to do nothing but advertise is a sure way to drive away your fan base.

If you already have people following you on social media platforms, you don't need to constantly try to sell to them. They already like your brand enough to take the time to follow you. Save the hard sell for people who are not customers yet. Better still; why not try a more subtle method?

Are you going to launch a new line of products soon or have a huge sale? Those things are certainly worth mentioning to your followers. However, avoid telling people too many times. Be sure to give them the information, and make all the details available. Beyond that, you don't need to beat everyone over the heads with your news. Instead of using social media to just throw advertising at people, try to engage them in a more meaningful way. Share wonderful content and find ways to interact with them in a way that is more enjoyable.

Removing Bad Comments

You are in control of your social media profiles. After some time, it's inevitable that people are going to leave negative feedback on your pages. It might seem all too easy to just delete those comments. Leaving those comments alone might seem like a highly damaging thing to do. However, you should think of each bit of bad feedback as a chance to do some damage control.

When someone makes a complaint on social media, it is a very public thing. Show people just how great your customer service skills are, by doing whatever it takes to make your unhappy followers happy again. You might not come out looking good every time. But simply dealing with negative comments as smoothly as possible will help to protect your image.

Let's suppose that you decide to just go ahead and delete bad comments instead. Do you think that it will stay a secret forever? Those customers will notice that you simply deleted their comments, and chose to ignore them. Even if you contacted them in private, they will feel jaded. It's likely that they will tell others about your little comment deleting habit. Soon, you might find that people don't trust your brand or you as a person.

Typos and Errors

You might not be able to hire someone to write your marketing content professionally. It's also true that people are more accepting with human errors, when it comes to social media. However, that is certainly no excuse to publish posts with grammar and spelling mistakes. If you post something with obvious errors, it might turn users away. At best, they will think that you are just a small time operation. At worst, they will think that you're not serious about being professional. You also run the risk of inviting the "grammar squad" to comment and fix your mistakes. It will draw attention away from the actual post.

Make sure that all of your information is also correct. This is especially important if you expect people to act upon that information. Before you press the button to publish something, stop for a moment and revise your content. Read over what you have written. If you are not sure about the quality of your own word, ask someone else to go over it for you again.

No matter who you are, or the size of your business, your posts need to be perfect. It doesn't matter that social media is generally a personal thing. Don't make the mistake of publishing content that contains a lot of mistakes.

Failing to Interact

Even if you choose to use an automatic poster to share your content, you need to be interacting with people. If you just share things and then seemingly disappear, ignoring any comment that people make, why bother in the first place. That type of behavior will soon lead people to view you as another advertiser, with no interest in social media.

If you actually take the time to interact with people, they will see you as more than just another cold-hearted business. They will realize that your company is run by people who have their own opinions and passions.

Fans will see that you care about customers and want to get to know them on a personal level. Social media is perfect for developing the kind of trust and engagement that was until recently only available to brick-and-mortar stores.

By reading what your fans think, and responding to them, it's possible to get some great ideas. When something isn't working well for customers, they are often happy to let you know about it. Of course, you can only benefit from this if you actually interact with them. Whatever you do, be sure to respond to feedback and comments, and check in on how your followers are doing.

Missing Your Call to Action

Maybe you have created the perfect series of posts across all of your social media marketing platforms. It could include a series of great images, videos, and text messages, that all tie in nicely with a new product you're launching. After posting it, imagine that you're not getting many sales conversions. Sure, people are interacting with your posts a lot. They're sharing them and commenting, plus you have loads of likes on every channel. What could the problem be?

Have you made sure to include a bullet-proof "call to action" on all of your posts? The call to action is just as it sounds. Once people have seen what you have to share, there needs to be something to tell them what to do next. For example, if you want people to visit your company website and look at your new product, be sure to make it easy! You have to call them into acting, by providing the necessary information. Tell them to visit your website and put the appropriate link in a place where they can't miss it.

It doesn't matter what you're trying to get people to do, make sure that you have a very clear call to action, on all of your marketing posts.

Posting Too Often

Sure, the people who follow your brand on social media probably want to hear from you on a regular basic. What they surely don't want is to be bombarded by way too many posts. No matter how loyal a customer is, they will eventually grow tired of this tactic. This book has recommend that you maintain a healthy amount of content, and even repost things regularly. That doesn't mean that you can just set up an automatic post to fire off every 15 minutes.

Be sure to show some self-control when you are posting on social media. Even if you have loads of new stuff to share with people, try to imagine that you are one of your fans. Before you post something, ask yourself if others will even want to see what you have to share. When people have to scroll past things that they just don't want to see, it's going to become very tempting to stop following you.

People who continuously post things that others don't want to see are called "spammers". They simply keep posting their content all over the place, as much as possible. Spammers don't care how many people they annoy, as long as they get as much exposure as possible. "Spam" is widely hated, and it often doesn't even work. Why would you want to risk turning your fans against you, for a so-called marketing tactic that doesn't even yield positive results.

Trying Too Hard to Be Relevant

Every time a big event, like a holiday or sports final comes around, social media goes absolutely crazy. It's safe to assume that marketers are taking these opportunities to try and relate their brands to whatever is happening at the time. This can be a very valuable tactic, but there are some pitfalls that you need to be mindful of.

Before you jump on the bandwagon with a big event, ask yourself if it's really relevant to what your brand is all about. If you are you selling men's shaving products, it might seem funny and cute to try and create a marketing campaign for mother's day. Hey, you might even manage to make it a success. Of course, there is the chance that people will think you're just trying too hard to seem relevant to the occasion.

If you try to force your brand into a big news story or a current event, people can usually tell. They don't tend to respond very well when this happens. Your company will look like it will do anything to try and sell to people. In addition to that, they might think that you believe your customers are stupid.

Trying to Be Everywhere

There are many, many different social media networks out there. That doesn't mean that you should try to use all of them at once. This type of thing will spread your attention too thin. Unless you have a huge team of people attending to them all, there's no way that you can be effective on every platform.

It is a better tactic to choose just a handful of networks. If you are just starting out, even focusing on one or two is perfectly acceptable. Try to work out which ones are best suited to your particular brand, and forget the rest for now. You are better off committing your resources to doing really well on just a few sites, instead of doing badly on lots of them.

Go to **"The Most Effective Social Media Platform for You"** and consider what your brand excels at. Try to choose some platforms that are at least a little different from each other. Even if you have mostly images to share, it's a mistake to only use Pinterest and Instagram. Choosing Facebook, Twitter, or both, is a good idea. They have the most fans at the moment, and most people you meet will probably have a profile with at least one of them.

Spending Too Much Time on Social Media

Don't forget that you have a business to run. If you want to be successful, it's important not to get sucked into the social media hole. It can take up an immense amount of time. People who are relatively new to marketing on social media can often get a little carried away. Once you get going, you can practically spend every hour of your waking life checking who commented on which post and how many followers you have gained today.

The very nature of social media means that it is constantly changing. Trying to stay up-to-date with what's happening all the time will only take over your life. You can soon start to feel like you need to respond instantly to avoid making people feel ignored. Staying connected and becoming obsessed are very different things. However, the line between them is dangerously thin. Don't become a social media junkie, or you might start to let your other areas of business slip.

PUTTING IT ALL TOGETHER: YOUR SOCIAL MEDIA PLAN

If you want to be successful at marketing your brand on social media, you have to be in this for the long haul. Don't expect to simply get started today and have thousands of loyal followers at the same time next week, or even next month. Yes, you will be able to see results by then, but the thing is, you need some time to put a good plan into action. That's what this chapter is all about: helping you to put the advice in this book into action, along with some added guidance.

The landscape for social media is constantly changing. Something that works well today might be different in six months' time. That doesn't mean that your expertise will become outdated. You simply need to maintain your knowledge and grow your plan as various networks change. There are always going to be basic fundamentals when it comes to marketing.

Creating Your Action Plan

People who make it big usually have a great plan to start with. Without one, you are essentially feeling around in the dark, hoping that you'll stumble upon something that works.

Step 1. Set Your Goals

Figure out what you wish to achieve through using social media. Did you just hear that "everyone needs to have a Facebook account", and decide to create a profile for your own brand. It's true that you should be using social media, as outlined in **"Why Social Media is so Influential"**. How you go about acting upon that need really does rely on what your goals are.

Write down what you want to get out of social media marketing. Maybe you would like to increase your sales, which is a common goal. How can you do that? A starting point might be driving more people to your business website. But what types of people would you like to go there. Surely you are looking for people who are interested in buying what you're selling. There's another goal that you can write down.

Maybe you're not trying to use social media to increase sales at all (which might be a big mistake, for your information). It could be that you would like to use some networks to increase your customer service, and give people a better quality of care after they have already purchased your goods or services. That's a perfectly acceptable goal, so write that down if it applies to your business.

Make your goals as specific as possible. Simply wanting to build a great social media network is too vague. How can you act upon something that isn't specific? In order to assess your success, those goals also need to be measurable. If you want to have a great network, what does that actually mean to you? Perhaps it means having at least 1,000 users on each of your chosen platforms after 6 months. That's a fairly modest, but also an attainable goal. That is the next part of setting good goals: making sure that they are actually doable. It's great to have high hopes, but it helps to be realistic about what you expect to accomplish. The final part of setting good goals is giving yourself a deadline. You might not actually get there in time, but at least you can plan your actions according to a schedule.

Whatever you do — do not get started with the next step until you have written down your goals.

Step 2. Choose Your Actions

Now that you know what you wish to achieve, through writing down your goals, it's time to figure out how to make them realities. How can you get what you want? This is where you find ways to turn your goals into actionable steps. If you want to direct more traffic to your website, how can you use social media to do so. For starters, you would want to use your posts to draw attention, engage people, and then show them a great call to action. That call to action would be, of course, visiting your website.

Before you can begin to achieve your goals, you will need to start with smaller steps. These include things like choosing which social media platforms you want to focus on. Next, you would need to create user accounts for your brand and place your branding media and information on them.

Think about metrics as well in this step. How many followers would you like to have in the coming months? It helps to create a yearly plan, then monthly and even a weekly plan. Work out what you will need to do, and when, in order to hopefully make your goals real.

As with any good action plan, you will need to assume that things won't always go according to plan. Allow some room for change, in case things do go wrong. Maybe you won't get as many followers as you had hoped. That could mean holding off on the next step a little longer, or even increasing the amount of resources that you put into gathering new fans.

Suggested Actions

You might not be sure what your actions should be. This book aims to deliver thorough instructions, so the actions below are suggested as a guide.

1. Choose which social media networks you want to use.

2. Sign up to them and complete your profiles fully.

3. Decide what kind of tone and image your brand will have on each individual network.

4. Plan a strategy for publishing posts (time, date, how often, etc.)

5. Test different formats and styles of post.

6. Analyze your test results.

7. Automate the process as much as possible, while still engaging users.

After you have completed these steps, start aiming higher by using the rest of this book as a guide for doing so. That means taking action steps to move toward your greater goals, as mentioned a little earlier in this chapter.

Step 3. Assess Your Social Media Accounts

If you are yet to set up your accounts, this step might not be too relevant just yet. However, this book is aimed at people who have a basic understanding of social media use already. If you're not using it for business yet, you can focus on your personal accounts as part of this experiment. Remember to record what you find and also any comments you have about your current usage. This will prove valuable later, when you are re-assessing your marketing plan.

You are going to basically "audit" your social media use. Take a look at what you have been doing so far. Has it been working to engage people? How many people have been connecting to you or interacting with posts you have published? If you don't take a look at your own techniques — before creating your plan — it will be all too easy to go down the wrong path.

You should now have a pretty good idea of some things that work, as well as those that don't seem to. This is where you can start to build up an archive of sorts. It will contain all your findings about things that do well for your business and those that don't. You can only learn so much by reading and asking for advice. There is also a lot to gain from real experience, so don't waste the opportunity to gain some insight.

Step 4. Create a Mission Statement

Unlike your goals and actions, a mission statement is relatively brief. In just a sentence or so, write a statement about what you want to achieve through social media marketing. This is separate from your business' mission statement, although the two will work to serve each other. In just a single sentence or so, write something that will help you focus on what you really want to get out of social media. This will become an invaluable tool in the future, when you are unclear about your purpose. If you have employees helping with social media marketing, it's a good idea to give each of them a copy of this mission statement. That way they will not be unsure about what their efforts are all about.

Step 5. Improving Your Social Media Accounts

Now that you have all the beginnings underway, it's time to improve things. You need to refine and enhance your presence on social media. At this point, you might have a better idea which networks are doing best. Maybe you have been heavily focusing on Twitter, but it doesn't seem to be giving you the kind of results you want. This is where you can either change your approach, or perhaps focus resources onto a different network, like Facebook for example.

You should also go over your profiles and make sure that they are as concise and effective as possible. Can you change your profile content to better attract customers? Are you using the right images, for example? Could you have a professional rewrite your text, to make it more effective? This is the time to start performing those little tweaks, now that you have a better idea of what you need to do. Start to polish everything on your social network accounts. Make sure that everything works as intended and try to make improvements wherever possible. It helps to have someone else give you a second opinion, especially if they have skills in social media use.

Step 6. Create Your Calendar

It can be tempting to just upload content as it's created. After all, if you've worked hard on something, you probably want to share it with people as soon as possible. While it can seem beneficial to put things out there quickly, you need to learn to schedule your posts properly. Using the advice given in the previous chapters of this book, you should know what kind of approach you want to take. Create a schedule of what you will post, and when. It helps to use automatic posting plugins or services for this, especially if you need to publish things overnight or on weekends.

Your calendar also needs to have times when you will check in on your social media accounts. Remember that you don't want to start checking them all obsessively. Have set times when you will go over everything, just as you would with any other aspect of your business.

Step 7. Keep Re-evaluating

Social media is a growing thing, almost like a living organism. There is no successful approach for people who are in the "set it and forget it" crowd. You're going to need to come back to this regularly to re-assess how things are going. You could choose to do this weekly in the beginning. After some time, once you are having more success, it might be easier to assess things once per month. Always check out your metrics and compare them to your desired goals. Make sure that you have been completing your required actions. Are they working well to bring you closer to your goals and mission statement? If so — that's great! If not, it is time to go back and see what is causing the problem. Identify what is working, and what is not. Tweak things where necessary. If you find that some more major reworking is needed, then carry it out.

SUMMARY

In summary, this book has now educated you in the best ways to implement a successful social media marketing plan. Just creating a profile and hoping that people come to you is not enough. There are always those who think that Facebook and Twitter are nothing more than places to throw advertisements at people. However, you now know better. It really isn't hard to get started. Doing it right is an ongoing effort though.

With the proper techniques, you can boost your sales for free, compete with even the biggest companies, interact with your customers in ways that were previously unheard of, check out what the competition is up to at all times, enjoy instant damage control, draw in customers who you never even knew existed and ensure that your business does not get left behind in this new age of technology.

There are a lot of different social media networks out there. It might seem like a good idea to just sign up to one and then leave things alone. On the other hand, maybe you used to think that signing up to all of them was the best option. Reading this has hopefully given you a much better understanding of how to properly focus your resources, thanks to the information in the second chapter of this book.

Knowing how to actually be a success on your chosen networks is a whole different story to just choosing the right ones to use. The strategies marked out in this book have given you a head start on your competition. You need to start with a great plan and then follow through until the end. This is an ongoing thing, so you can't just set it up and forget about it. It takes experimentation and you can spend some money to make things easier. Tracking your data and usage is always important, so don't forget about that step.

Once you become more comfortable with using social media, you can try to draw people in with your own special events. Likewise, you can focus on drawing attention from influential people in social media. Using their popularity, you might be able to get some extra attention for your own brand. In time, you will hopefully be a big influence yourself.

Before you start to go too far with your planning, become familiar with all of the mistakes that you might make. Some things seem like great ideas to the beginner, however, by learning from the experience of others, you can avoid doing things the wrong way.

Once you have your plan ready to go, begin to put it into action. You will need to keep monitoring your progress and recording your metrics and data. Use that information to work out how well your plan is doing which will help you to make changes in the future.

Learning how to successfully market your brand on social media is complex. There is a lot of competition out there and many people have already made it. However, with the information in this book, and a will to persevere — you can become a social media marketing success!

ABOUT THE AUTHOR

Brad Jones is an internet marketer and digital entrepreneur. He now makes a 6 figure income by working online for myself running multiple businesses.

He started experimenting with earning money online back in 2002 on the side, whilst he continued working his 9-5 sales job. It wasn't until 2008 that he finally got to the point where his side income covered his monthly expenses, and he saw the opportunity to earn a lot more. He quit his job later that year and has been working for himself ever since.

Brads believes there are many people claiming how to make money online, and in his experience there is no ONE best way. He's found success in many avenues, and believes it's down to the individual's passions and interests that will produce the best results for them.

Brad has written several books demonstrating some of the ways you can make a living working online, and he's have found success in all of them.

"Be open to try new things, never quit, and you'll find the success you're looking for. I promise you!"

MORE BOOKS BY BRAD JONES

Blogging Brilliance – How to A Make Bundle on Your Blog

Ebay Excellence – Making Easy Money the Ebay Way

Fiverr Freedom – From Your First Gig to Making A Fortune On Fiverr

Flawless Freelance Writing – How to Make A Fortune Freelance

Storytelling – A Storytelling System to Deliver Inspiring and Unforgettable Speeches

You're The Problem – 30 Real Life Solutions to Stop Destructive Actions and Get Out of Your Own Way

www.ingramcontent.com/pod-product-compliance
Lightning Source LLC
Chambersburg PA
CBHW071019180526
45168CB00003B/1483